CRETAN SPORTS ASSOCIATION

MARKETING PLAN 2015-2016

MICHAEL KASSOTAKIS

SCOTLAND, UNITED KINGDOM, SPRING, 2000-2015

TABLE OF CONTENTS 2

1.0 <u>EXECUTIVE SUMMARY</u>

Cretan Sports Association is a fictitious not for profit organization that provides the community with learning, team and sports activities. It is the premier provider of youth experiences and serves more than 30,000 participants in four sports (football, basketball, volleyball and gymnastics) throughout the Iraklion area with potential participation from other areas of Crete. Participants include public, private and home school students.

Our marketing focus, made explicit in this plan, renews our vision and strategic focus on adding quality to our program and making it affordable and available for all interested participants. This can be achieved through successful fund-raising activities, our experienced coaches, volunteers and personnel and a solid financial approach to managing our resources.

C.S.A will have to confront uncertainties related to government policies, facility, human resources and fund requirements as well as the impact of alternative programs. All the people who are involved in the C.S.A activities will continue to work optimistically and effectively toward improving the quality of the program and making the association exceptional in the services it offers.

2.0 **MISSION AND OBJECTIVES**

The goal of the C.S.A is to create a favourable environment that enhances self-confidence and self-control through experiences in sports activities. It is dedicated to provide all Cretan youth with superior quality learning and team experience through sports participation. The involvement of young people in the youth sports program offers them the opportunity to develop a wide range of skills such as teamwork, interaction with others, sportsmanship and fair play.

The objective is to provide all these benefits to as many children as possible in a creative and positive manner. The sought-after-result of the youth sports program is a meaningful and constructive experience. More specifically the C.S.A, through this plan, intends to achieve the following objectives:

- Provide a positive experience to 32,000 youth through the academic year 2015-2016.
- Expand the program to two new schools within our serving area, prior to the 2015-2016 academic years.
- Raise a minimum of $1000000000 through non-participation fees from sources including donations, contributions, special events, gifts-in-kind and grants.
- Accomplish our program goals within the allocated budget.

3.0 **PRODUCT/MARKET BACKGROUND**

C.S.A offers young people the opportunity to take part in a variety of team sports throughout the year. The participation in these sports improves athletic skills, health and fitness and provides learning experiences in teamwork, sportsmanship, fair play cooperation and leadership. The target segments of the C.S.A are the public, private and home school students. The growth rate is 5-7% for the public school segment, 3-4% for the private school segment and 2-3% for the home school segment. The program has experienced an average annual growth rate of 5-6% for the past five years. This indicates the growing needs of the market (See Appendix 7.1 Target Market Forecast). The most dramatic growth is expected in the basketball programs with relative static participation expected in other sports.

3.1 Market demographics

C.S.A serves the Iraklion area with a total population in excess of 200,000 people. An estimated 14.6 of the population contains children between the ages of 5-19. Therefore an estimated 58,400 children between the ages of 5-19 are potential C.S.A participants. An estimate of 60% of the participants is male and 40% female. Boys dominate football and basketball and girls volleyball.

Furthermore, the parents of the participants work full time (8 hours per day) have more than one child living at home and their time is limited. They appreciate the physical and social skills their child receives through the youth sports program.

Finally, the local community supports solidly the concept and the purpose of the organization (See Appendix 7.2: Market trends).

3.2 Market needs

School-sponsored sports programs are limited in terms of age and range of events. The public school system fails to offer sufficient quality standards in sports programs. A lot of sports programs have not survived due to limited school funding and increasing economic pressures on the public school system. C.S.A serves all children from kindergarten through high schools no matter what the school they attend offers. The only requirement for them is the desire to participate.

4. O SITUATION ANALYSIS

According to various studies, there is a direct value of youth participation in sports. This study indicate that the young people who participate in sports activities have less chances to get involved in smoking, drug, sex crime, and other anti-social behaviour. C.S.A approves all these research findings and offers long-term personal and social values to participants throughout their lives. It adopts the notion that "investing" on young people results in a more developed community.

4.1 SWOT Analysis

The following outlines the most significant strengths and weaknesses internal to C.S.A and the opportunities and threats that exist in our external environment.

Strengths

-C.S.A goodwill-C.S.A enjoys a positive perception within the community. It is considered to have a positive influence on youth and the potential deterrent to violence and other anti-social behaviour. More and more families want to send their children to participate in the programme.

-Access to facilities-public and private schools, local churches, football clubs, basketball clubs and other sports organisations offer their athletic facilities (gyms, football fields, and basketball fields) to the C.S.A.

-Donor base- the donor base comes from both private and public sources. It is stable and loyal.

Weaknesses

-Facilities-in the future the existing facilities may be insufficient due to increase in programme needs and recent restrictions and fees for the use of sports fields.

-Financial resources- the completion of our sports programme depends partially on revenues from participants and traditional fund raising events. Additional funds are needed due to increasing programme needs.

-Human resources- the increase in reputation as well as the increasing participation in the C.S.A sport activities has caused great pressure to the staff of the C.S.A. this results in turnover in some positions.

Opportunities

-Geographic expansion- surrounding communities show increasing interest for the sports activities of C.S.A. this may open new revenue opportunities.

-Programme expansion- the current programme can be expanded by adding new sports to the current venue. Adult sports programmes can be included.

Threats

-Alternative programmes- there are sports clubs that offer specific programmes according to their specialisation (football, basketball, volleyball). They target skilled players and coaches. This is a major threat for the participants and the coach resources of the C.S.A.

-Health and safety issues- the wide range and the nature of sports activities that the C.S.A offers demands constant watch on the health and safety of the participants. There is always the danger of an injury that may affect the reputation of the C.S.A.

-Political issues- the government policy may restrict the ability of local public school to offer their facilities for use by C.S.A.

<u>Competition</u>

There is no significant competitor in Crete. Some sports clubs offer specific attributes but no one offers the extensive range of experiences or infra structure of the

C.S.A. the C.S.A is the leader in the market. Its market share is more than 65%. This is based on the estimated number of participants compared to participation programmes in other levels both private and public.

5.0 **MARKETING STRATEGIES**

C.S.A's strategy is to be the market leader in the provision of sports experiences in the area served. The focus will be in offering the participants superior quality sports programmes with minimal costs. Experienced coaches, staff and executives as well as the strong donor based and the community supporters are the key success factors of this focus.

Furthermore, the marketing strategy attempts to successfully communicate the unique value the programme offers to participants. It will continue to identify the needs of the market and communicate with the participants and their guardians in the most effective and positive manner possible. C.S.A will continue to develop the quality and efficiency of the programme through improvements and changes in its structure and implementations.

Finally, C.S.A will investigate the opportunities to expand the participation in the programmes in adult segments and other geographic areas of Crete (Chania, Rethymno and Lassithi). This will be based on the continuous attention to the quality of the sports and social experience that the C.S.A provides as well as on the availability of sports facilities in other geographic areas.

5.1 Target strategy

For the purpose of this plan the target market will be young people between the ages of five and eighteen. These young people are mainly private public and home school students who are interested in participating in competitive sports. In the future adults will be another target segment.

5.2 Positioning strategy

C.S.A cooperates with parents and the local community to provide all youth with the highest quality education and team experience through sports participation. All young people can participate in one or more sports no matter what their previous experience skill level or athletic ability is. The breadth, depth of overall quality of the sports experience we offer can not be matched within our market.

5.3 Marketing Mix

Product

C.S.A is a not for profit organisation that offers sports opportunities that are an integral part of each participants learning experience. The C.S.A is dedicated to offer the following services to each participant:

- The opportunity to develop creative skills through participation in organised team sports.
- A means to experience a variety of sports.
- Development of team work, sportsmanship, fair play and athletic skills.
- A means to enhance their health and fitness and increase their self-confidence.

- A source of fun and enjoyment to enrich their lives.
- Supervision and teaching during the day. Parents can realise the benefits of saving time and offering learning experiences to their children.

Price

C.S.A will charge the participants with fees of 30 Euros per month in order to cover costs and provide additional revenue for service levels to be maintained or to grow. This price is the cheapest compared with the price that other competitive organisations charge. It is a source of competitive advantage. Methods of payment would be flexible (deeds of covenant, provision of goods or services, credit cards, membership/subscription fees etc.) in order to facilitate participation and fund raising from the community.

Promotion

The promotion strategy will be extensive in order to generate participation and fund raising. The methods that will be used include:

-Campaigns that utilise mass and specialist media advertising.

-Television appeals with celebrities and telephone hot lines for instant donations by credit cards.

-Direct mail to selected target groups who maybe pass donors who belong to special interest groups.

-Personal selling. Special professionals will deal with major organisations that are potential donors. Door to door and street collections will also be used.

-Use of Internet. The creation of a website and e-mail facility will help the association to deliver directly information and communicate with the community.

-Association brochure and newsletter. The management team will develop an association brochure to explain the benefits of membership to prospective members and associate members. The newsletter (along with fax and e-mail notices) will improve the flow in critical information and raise the awareness of the association.

-Public relations. C.S.A will establish relationships with key individuals and organisations that desire to provide significant financial support on an ongoing basis. Furthermore the association will lobby the government in order to gain support for its goals.

Place (distribution)

The association will deal directly with its target segments in order to provide its services. The major task in distribution management will be to ensure the availability and accessibility of services. At the moment this is achieved by the geographic proximity among the establishment of C.S.A, its facilities, participants and sponsors. In the future, as the program will be expanded in other geographic areas, a network of branches and central basis in major cities will be established in order to serve the participants and manage fund raising and other activities.

People

C.S.A offers people-based services. The staff has high contact with the participants and sponsors. This means that skilled coaches, volunteers and executives have to be retained or recruited in order to maintain or enhance the quality of the program and raise more funds.

6.0 **CONTROLS**

The purpose of the C.S.A marketing plan is to serve as a guide to the staff, the board of directors and the volunteers to continue to improve the organisation and its ability to serve the youth of Crete. We will track plan versus actual resorts of the program on order to evaluate it at our Board of Directors meetings. The program will be revised if we discover that it does not accomplish the intended goal.

Our organisation has one paid staff person who has key responsibilities in marketing implementation. This person will attend all Board of Directors meetings to report the status and the progress of the program and will chair the monthly meetings of the Marketing Committee.

Finally some of the key variables that would be monitored in order to guarantee the high quality of the program and its financial return are:

-Market growth rate and our fund raising growth compared to it.

-Market share and share changes of all the competitive organisations in the market.

-Surplus margins as a percent of fund raising.

-Number of participants who are new to our program.

-Turnover rates of coaches, volunteers and staff.

-Coaches and volunteers opinions about association support and feeling of empowerment.

-Number of complaints and resolved complaints.

7.0 APPENDICES

APPENDIX 7.1

TARGET MARKET FORECAST

Potential customers	Growth	2015	2016	2017
Public school students	5-7%	30000	31500 - 32100	33075 - 33705
Private school students	3-4%	4000	4120 - 4160	4244 - 4284
Home school students	2-3%	800	816 - 824	832 - 840
Total	5-6%	34800	36436 - 37084	38151- 38829

APPENDIX 7.2

MARKET TRENDS

The most important market trends are the following:

-Corporations and individuals are interested in sponsoring and supporting sports activities when they receive benefits such as tax benefits and social prestige.

-The community is increasingly aware that involvement in sports reduces the potential for anti-social behaviour.

-The government reduces its financial support to public schools for sports activities.

APPENDIX 7.3

KEYS TO SUCCESS

-Identify additional facilities to support future growth and offer greater flexibility in scheduling.

-Expand to new areas within the island of Crete that desire access to our sports activities.

-Be perceived by public private and home schooling providers as a valuable resource that compliments the academic experiences they offer.

-Continue to develop the donor base and corporate contributions that adds to the financial resources of the participant fees.

-Continue to offer programs that are perceived to be positive, in enriching and affordable compared to the alternatives in our area.

APPENDIX 7.4

FINANCIALS

C.S.A will emphasise on reducing the reliance on fee-based revenues and look toward contributions for other sources such as fund raising, charitable gifting and tournaments. This approach will enable the program to realise the objective of keeping fees affordable while continuing to offer a quality program for all participants.

The following summarises key factors regarding the financial status of C.S.A and its 2009 results (2009 Independent Auditor's Report):

-Revenues in 2009 totaled $1500000.

-A total of 65% of those revenues are from Participation Fees, Donations and Contributions, Special Events and Gifts-in-Kind.

-Supervision grants account for a combined 33%.

-Expenses for 2009 where almost equal to revenues.

-"People-related" expenditures represent 44% of expenditures.

-Non program operations account for 8% of the total expenditures.

Furthermore the breakeven analysis offers general insight regarding the number of average participants we must have involved in the program each month.

Breakeven Analysis

Assumptions:

Average Per-Unit Revenue	30.00 Euros
Average Per-Unit Variable Cost	12.9
Estimated Fixed Costs*	10260
Monthly Units Breakeven	600
Monthly Revenue Breakeven	18000

*Fixed costs include the building lease, payroll, utilities and marketing costs. This number is due to our dependence on volunteers to run our program.

Finally, the funding forecast for the 2015-2016 academic year will fluctuate based on the seasonality of the sports offered and the projected level of participation in each sport. The forecasted revenues will range from $33,000 in September as schools are getting started to $220,000 in November with a lot of tournaments overlapping.

APPENDIX 7.5

CONTIGENCY PLANNING

The marketing plan will be modified if one of the following changes occurs:

-Rapid growth of one of the alternative programmes that significantly reduces our market share.

-Injury or negligence that causes severe financial damage to the organisation. This means legal action.

-Major philosophy shift regarding the use of public and/or private school facilities.

APPENDIX 7.6

7.6.1 Globalization

"The globalization of markets is at hand…the global corporation operates with resolute constancy…as if the entire world (or major regions of it) were a single entity; it sells the same things in the same way everywhere" (Levitt 1983:92).

One of the most significant economic developments since World War II is the increasing globalization of business. Although business has been conducted across national boundaries for centuries (Fortune, 1988), during the last decades business dealings have been developed on a global scale. The global increase of international business affects the world economic environment profoundly (Fortune, 1992). Leading corporations around the world have increasingly turned their attention to international business in order to expand and maintain a competitive advantage in today's dynamic economic scale. International businesses refer to a wide range of activities involved in conducting business transactions across national boundaries. The internationalization of marketing and manufacturing activity (Business Week, 1994) has become important even for small companies in order to sustain growth and profitability. Sales for firms with no foreign activities grow faster in every industry and profitability also rises for firms with a broad global scope. In the past two decades, international companies have shifted from production-oriented concerns to building long term partnerships all over the world (Yip, 1995).

The implementation of the marketing concept on a global scale, means understanding the consumer. Nowadays, consumers become more and more sophisticated and informed about global products. Global marketing needs to be integrated in order to meet complex global consumer needs. As a result world markets will be more sophisticated and informed and globalized in the current millennium. Global businesses will be expanded due to the following needs:

- Economies of scale consideration will push more companies toward producing or selling abroad (Business Week, 1994). Non-domestic markets will provide many international firms with corporate earnings growth.

- The progressive homogenization of home country management with that of the host country will bring the adoption of global business (Bartlett and Choshal,

1991). Global businesses will allocate more of their corporate resources to their international divisions.

- Tremendous similarities in consumption and buying patterns will result in the emergence of a standardized global culture enforced by the help of mass media (Usunier, 1996).

- Growth in international company operations and increased organizational orientation towards globalization will create a positive environment for global products.

- The creation of world products will demand a global marketing approach that uses standardized marketing strategies (Douglas and Craig, 1989). For example companies will try to develop advertising messages that can appeal to people across national boundaries.

- Firms recognize the threat of the intensification of competition and the opportunity of universal homogenized need (Yip, 1995). So they design global marketing plans in order to support the production of global products for global consumers.

- The combination of low costs, superior quality and reliability incorporated with identical design and function can overcome any kind of barriers. Failure in globalization is recorded only when there is failure I execution or failure in marketing imagination (Levitt, 1983).

- Thanks to modern information, communication and transportation technology, the world is driven towards a converging commonality (Levitt, 1983). The result is the emergence of global markets.

- Successive rounds of agreements have lowered tariffs since World War II. At the same time, regional economic agreements such as the European Union have facilitated trade relations among member countries (Yip, 1995).

In conclusion, global companies that show sensitivity to the long-range planning, desires of consumers, continuous R&D, innovative orientation and establishment of global relationships will guarantee their success in global markets of the future. (Kaynak, 1985).

7.6.2 The Process of Globalization

The internationalization process can be described by various schools of thoughts. Most of them focus on particular issues of the process rather than on the process on the whole. These include the Uppsala, Transaction cost, Strategic, Porter's Paradigm, Eclectic Paradigm and the network model which are analyzed below.

Uppsala Approach

The Uppsala model focuses on which market and form of entry is chosen by firms when going abroad. There is a distinction among four different modes of entering an international market, where the successive stages represent higher degrees of geographic diversification and international involvement and market commitment.

Stage 1: no regular export activities

Stage 2: export via independent representatives

Stage 3: establishment of a foreign sales subsidiary

Stage 4: foreign production and manufacturing units

So firms prefer to initiate the process with forms that require low commitment (exporting, licensing) and then try to carry out F.D.I. (Foreign Direct Investment) and establish branches (Johanson and Wiedersheim-Paul 1975; Johanson and Vahlne, 1977).

Transaction cost approach

This approach analyzes the internationalization of firms from the point of view of transaction cost economics. Firms internationalize when transaction costs inside the organization are lower than their costs in the market. Intangible assets such as technology and knowhow are very important in the decision to internationalize as well as in the selection of the most appropriate mode to do so. The technology and know-how provide the necessary potential to enter new markets. The firm can internalize the international operations, for example establishment of foreign branches, when the volume of the assets involved is high (Teece, 1986, Klein et al, 1990).

The strategic approach

According to the strategic approach, internationalization is derived from the adoption of strategies that take into consideration the strengths and weaknesses of the firm as well as the opportunities and threats of the environment. It refers mainly to multinationals, which have already undertaken international activities on various countries. Furthermore, it focuses on explaining the form of internationalization and the organizational structure of the different units and branches of the company (Doz, 1986; Ghoshal 1987).

Porter's Paradigm

This paradigm analyses how national conditions affect firm's competitive advantage in international markets. Firms that follow the pathway of internationalization have to take into consideration the following aspects.

Demand conditions. The competitive position of a firm is affected by demand characteristics in the host country.

Supporting activities. Supporting industries and activities restrict or enhance the capabilities of the firm at a particular country or location. This is one of the most important national resources for some sectors.

Firm resources. In an international environment the firm's competence is influenced by the degree of development of the firm's resource such as financial, human or infrastructure resources.

Competition intensity. The degree of competition influences the firm's innovative capabilities competitive advantage and strategy to a long extent (Porter, 1990).

The Eclectic Paradigm

According to the scheme proposed by the eclectic paradigm there are two groups of factors that affect foreign direct investment and the decision to enter foreign markets. The internationalization of economic activity is decided by the realization of location and ownerships advantages. The location advantages arise when it is better to combine products manufactured in the home country with intermediate products manufactured in another country. The ownership advantage relate to the integration of transactions into international hierarchies through foreign direct investment. They are derived from the firm's ability to manage activities internally in the value added chain (Dunning, 1997).

The network model

However, the network model is considered as the most appropriate approach, which can describe the internationalization process of small sport firms.

Small sport firms develop multiple relationships for international activities in order to exploit them across different markets. These firms internationalize rapidly and don't follow step by step approaches like their larger counterparts. Furthermore, they emphasize on the use of relationships to identify foreign market opportunities and undertake international activities.

Networks are an emerging approach as an organizational structure appropriate to sport associations that plan to globalize their activities. These firms are characterized by entrepreneurial ventures (Dubini and Aldrich, 1991). The development of small sport firms tends to be dependent on relationships with others. These relationships include customers, suppliers, competitors, private and public support agencies (Axelson, and Easton, 1992).

Thus the nature and integration of relationships with others in the market can initiate the firm's ability to internationalize and broaden its global strategic options. Firms can expand from domestic to international markets through existing or developing relationships, that offer contacts and facilitates the development of new partners and positions in the new markets (Johanson and Mattsson 1988). These relationships can help to overcome barriers in market entry and international activities.

In conclusion the internationalization process of a small sport firm can be facilitated if we examine the firm's role and position with a network of relationships. Network contacts, rather than decisions, taken solely by managers in the firm, initiate foreign market selection and entry. When network contacts either formal (e.g. business related) or informal (i.e. friends) match with the market and the product characteristics of the firm, then it can rapidly be involved in the foreign markets and undertake international activities (Covielo and Munro, 1993).

The form of international market development relies on the network relationships for marketing related activities. Managers of entrepreneurial firms should pay attention to how and with whom these relationships are established. Although, marketing control over operations maybe wakened, because of loss of touch with multiple market dynamics and the development of multiple relationships, they are considered very vital in gaining market access and supplementing their marketing weakness. Continuous market research can facilitate control in relationships and performance evaluation of linkage partners. Finally, managers can strengthen the competitive advantage of their small sport firms by developing the existing networks and establishing new ones. This can broaden the range of strategic options available and the various resources that are necessary for the accomplishment of the selected strategies.

Bibliography, References

Axelsson, B. and Easton, G. (1992) "Industrial Networks: A View of Reality",
Routledge, London.

Bartlett, C and Ghoshal, S. (1991), "Global strategic management: the impact on the new
frontiers of strategy research" Strategic Management Journal, Vol. 12, pp. 5-16

Business Week (1994), "New worlds to conquer" February 28.

Covielo, N.E. and Munro, H. J. (1993) "Linkage development and the role of marketing
in the internationalization of the entrepreneurial high technology firm" in Hills.

Doz, Y. (1986) "Strategic Management in Multinational Companies" Pergamon Press,
Oxford.

Douglas, S.P. and Craig, C.S. (1989), "Evolution of global marketing strategy: scale,
scope, synergy", Columbia Journal of World Business, Autumn, pp. 47-58.

Fortune (1988), "How to be a global manager", March 14, p 52.

Fortune (1992), "Do you know where your Ford was made?", June 17, p 53.

Fortune (1989), "How to go global and why", August 17, p 70.

Hollensen, S., 1998, Global Marketing – A market-response approach, Prentice Hall

Johanson, J. and Wiedersheim-Paul, (1975), The internationalization of the firm-four
Swedish cases, Journal of Management Studies, October, pp. 305-322.

Johanson J. and Vahlne, J.E. (1977) "The internationalization process of the firm: a
model of knowledge development and increasing foreign market commitment, Journal of
International Business Studies, Vol 8, No 1, pp. 23-32.

Kotler, P. (1997). Marketing Management, 9th edition, Prentice Hall, New Jersey.

Levitt, T. (1983), "The Globalization of Markets", Harvard Business Review, Vol. 61, pp. 92-102.

McDonald M. and Wilson H. (2011) "Marketing Plans, How to Prepare Them, How to Use Them, 7th ed, Wiley.

Porter, M.E. (1990), "The Competitiveness of Nations" Free Press, New York.

Teece, D.J. (1986), "Transaction cost economics and the multinational enterprise", Journal of Economic Behaviour and Organisation, Vol. 7, pp 21-45.

Usunier, J.C. (1996) "Marketing across cultures", Prentice Hall.

Yip, G.S. (1995), "Total global strategy: managing for worldwide competitive advantage", Prentice Hall, Englewood Cliffs, NJ

www.ingramcontent.com/pod-product-compliance
Lightning Source LLC
Chambersburg PA
CBHW072030190526
45166CB00015B/1761